Notes to Self

Notes to Self

Vol 1 : Love, Reflection, and Them

Frank Medina III

AuthorHouse™
1663 Liberty Drive
Bloomington, IN 47403
www.authorhouse.com
Phone: 1-800-839-8640

First published by AuthorHouse 06/22/2011

ISBN: 978-1-4634-0999-9 (sc)
ISBN: 978-1-4634-0998-2 (ebk)

Library of Congress Control Number: 2011909574

Printed in the United States of America

This book is a compilation of thoughts and emotions. A scratch book of my story, dedicated to those who have influenced me . . . both positive and negative . . .

Prologue

"ROCKSTAR" VS "THINKER"

I'm going to start by saying. This isn't a biography (that's in the works, but the end is yet to be lived). This isn't a poetry book either. This is a gathering of my thoughts! A form of therapy you can say. Sometimes the only way, I can express myself is through lyrics and words.

I believe everyone has two sides. Both my sides have seen a lot. My sides tend to conflict as well. On the one hand, you have the happy go-lucky party animal. This guy is called "Rock star". And that's how he lives. Life is like a movie to him. He makes others believe he's at a level, he only wishes one day to obtain. This is very common for people, who grew up in my area (Washington Heights).This side has gotten into trouble at times. Trouble that he hasn't been able to let go . . .

The second side to this man is probably the complete opposite from the first. This side is the "Deep—thinker". This side can create; this side can imagine, this side feels he can change the world! This side is usually melancholy, and monotone. That's because this side is usually sad. You see this side is over shadowed, by the "Rock star". Everyone only notices the "Rock star". Out here no one cares what you think. So it doesn't matter that in the 4th grade he was writing short-stories at a high school level. This side isn't just Washington Heights, this side can relate to the WHOLE WORLD! Deep down I want to be this side, 90 percent of the time. But what would be the point? People just see the "Rock star". It's a losing battle between the two. The "Thinker" lost a lot because of the "Rock star". He lost his love, he lost his chance of meeting people who related to him, at one point he lost himself. And he wasn't able to do what he does best (again; create, imagine, etc).

So what can be done about this confliction? The "Thinker" can't beat the "Rock star". No way no how, I am the "Rock star". No I'm not, I'm the "Thinker". Unless the "Thinker" can use the "Rock star", to get what he wants. You see the "Thinker" is always going to be smarter than the "Rock star". And the "Rock star" can get the "Thinker" into places he would never be able to go.

So that's the answer! One will use the other, than they can both live in HARMONY! Because when all is said and done, at the end of the day . . . to achieve true happiness is to live without regret, realize your faults, and know who you are! I am the "Rock star", but even more than that I am the "Thinker". The "Thinker", who can see the world through the eyes of a select few and bring it to you. Ladies and gentleman, I now introduce you to the "THINKER".

PART 1

REFLECTION

SOMETHING'S MISSING

I LOOK, BUT CAN'T FIND IT . . .
CAN'T GET IT FROM THE ONE INFRONT OR THE ONE BEHIND IT
WHAT IS THAT I'M MISSING?
THAT WON'T EVEN GET YOU THINKING
OR MAYBE TRY TO LISTEN . . .
MY IMPRESSIONS LEAD TO MISLEADING PERCEPTIONS
OVER REACTED ACCUSATIONS AND REJECTION
NOT TO MENTION FALSE PRETENCES AND MISCONCEPTION
WHAT CAN I DO?
IM JUST BEING ME, NOT TRYING TO LIVE THROUGH YOU
BECAUSE MOST OF YOU ARE FULL OF SHITT, AND I AM LIVING PROOF
OF WHAT HAPPENS WHEN YOU GET SHITT DONE TO YOU . . .
WHEN YOUR HEART WAS BROKEN OR YOUR FACE WAS BEATENED TOO
WHEN YOUR LIFE WAS ALMOST TAKEN
AND YOU'RE JUST TRYING TO MAKE IT THROUGH
WHEN YOU'VE BEEN TOLD YOUR WRONG, KNOWING THAT IT'S TRUE!

SO MAYBE THERE'S NOTHING LOST, MAYBE NOTHING IS MISSING
MAYBE I COULD FIND IT, IF YOU COULD TAKE A SECOND

REJECTION

REJECTION . . .
WHAT IS REJECTION?
REJECTION IS NOT HAVING A PERCEPTION ON WHO YOU ARE!
IF YOU KNOW WHO YOU ARE, YOU CAN NEVER BE REJECTED!
BECAUSE IF ONE DOOR IS CLOSED, ANOTHER IS OPENED!
IF SOMEONE TELLS YOU NO, THE OTHER OPENS THEIR ARMS . . .
IF YOU BELIEVE IN YOURSELF, REJECTION IS MERELY A FORK IN THE ROAD
REJECTION IS A FORM OF PROTECTION, AGAINST YOURSELF . . .
IT ALLOWS YOU TO QUIT, AND NEVER KNOW THE TRUTH . . .
CAN IT BE DONE OR CAN'T IT BE DONE?
REJECTION IS DETECTION, ON WHO AND WHAT IS REAL!
MOST OF ALL REJECTION, MEANS THEY AINT WORTH THE SHITT!

HOW?

HOW CAN I ERASE, MY MISTAKES?
REPLACE ALL THAT HATE THAT CONSUMES ME
AND ONE DAY MAY LEAD TO MY FATE
HOW CAN I UNDO, WAT IS MISCONSTRUED?
AND WHAT PEOPLE DON'T SEE
BUT OFTEN ASSUME
HOW CAN I TAKE BACK, WHAT ONCE WAS MINE?
WHAT NO LONGER IS
BUT STILL I TRY
HOW CAN I SEE THE TRUTH THAT IS?
THAT ALWAYS WAS
AND JUST LETS ME LIVE
MOST OF ALL
HOW CAN I RISE WHEN I FALL?
DUST OFF MY SHOULDERS
AND PUSH THREW IT ALL!

HOLES

ITS LIKE A HOLE
EMPTINESS AND VOID
THAT YOU CAN'T AVOID
IT PROBABLY FEELS THE SAME
FOR THE GIRLS AND BOYS
ITS WHAT U GET
WHEN YOU'RE DONE WITH TOYS, AND GAMES
AND EVERYTHING ELSE JUST FEELS THE SAME
YOU SWARE YOU CAN MANTAIN
BUT IT LINGERS ON YOUR BRAIN
U START TO REFELCT
WHETHER IT'S BETTER TO BE LOVED
OR TO HAVE RESPECT!
OR IF YOU CAN DO WITH ONE AND STILL FEEL NEGLECT . . .
AND YOU WISH YOU HELD ON TO WAT YOU HAD, CAUSE IT WASNT SO SAD . . .
IT WASN'T SO WRONG, IT WASN'T THAT BAD . . .

FEAR

I FEAR THE WORSE
I FEAR THINGS I CAN'T CONTROL
I DONT FEAR DEATH! BUT I FEAR GROWING OLD . . .
I DON'T FEAR LOVE, BUT I FEAR I WILL NEVER FEEL IT AGAIN
I FEAR, THAT I MAY FEAR TO THE VERY END
I FEAR THE PAST I FEAR THE FUTURE
I DON'T FEAR THE PRESENT BUT IT GETS CLOSER EACH SECOND
I FEAR I COULD DO THINGS A LITTLE DIFFERENT
I FEAR IM NOT THAT PERSISTENT
I FEAR MY OWN INSECURITIES BUT I DON'T FEAR THEY CAN BURY ME
I FEAR THAT I MADE TOO MANY MISTAKES I FEAR THERE'S TO MANY RISKS I TAKE
MOST OF ALL I I FEAR THAT I CAN NEVER FEEL
THE WAY I FELT, WEN U WERE NEAR . . .

THROUGH THE LOOKING GLASS

THROUGH THE LOOKING GLASS . . .
LIKE ALICE N WONDERLAND
DRINK THIS LIL CUP . . .
THEN MAYBE U CAN UNDERSTAND . . .
WHAT'S GOD'S PLAN . . .
IT IS IN HIS HANDS
WHEN UP IS DOWN, AND DOWN IS UP
AND NUTIN MAKES SENSE
AND YOU JUST DON'T GIVE A FUCK
DO WE MAKE OUR OWN LUCK?
CAN I FIT THROUGH THIS RABBIT HOLE . . .
OR WILL I GET STUCK?

Paid a Price

Sick and tired
Of being sick and tired
Dealing with the fakes,
Haters and liars . . .
Putting my hand in the fire
Knowing, that it's wrong
Knowing the record's old
But still playing the song
What the hell is going on?
Can't anything go right
Is it something I'm doing wrong
Or is that simply life?
Wish I could do it twice
I don't have any regrets
But my actions . . .
Paid a price

I'M AN ALIEN

I MUST BE FROM OUTERSPACE
EVERY WHERE I TURN, I FEEL IM OUT OF PLACE
YOU CAN SEE IT ON MY FACE
IM DISGUSTED BY THE HATE, THE FAKES
THE LIES N DECEIT, I TURN AND RETREAT
DON'T UNDERSTAND HOW IT IS THEY SPEAK
ABOUT THE SAME BS, THAT WON'T HELP THEM TO PROGRESS!
THEY OUT TO BE A WORKER
BUT NEVER STRIVE TO BE A BOSS!
HOPEFULLY SOON, I CAN GET LOST!
AND RETURN BACK TO WHERE I BELONG!

WUDNT THINK TWICE

ON NIGHTS LIKE THIS, I SIT AND REMINISCE
AS I SIP THIS DRINK, AND SMOKE THIS SHITT
WONDER ‡THE WAT IF'S·, REMEMBER MY FIRST KISS
THINK ABOUT THE CHICKS, AND WAS IT WORTH¿
WOULD I GO BACK, DO IT ALL THE SAME¿
IF I DID IT DIFFERENT, WOULD IT STILL MAINTAIN¿
ON THE OTHERSIDE, IM NOT THAT OTHER GUY
WE ARE WHO WE ARE
BEING ME HAS GONE PRETTY FAR
STILL I WISH UPON A STAR
THE MONEY AND THE CARS
FAME AND THE FORTUNE
IS THAT WHAT WE LIVE FOR¿
IS IT WORTH THE PRICE¿
YET WHAT WOULD I GIVE FOR A CHANCE
TO SEE ANOTHER LIFE
AND TO FIND THAT PEACE
I WUDN'T THINK IT TWICE

LIVING IN THE PAST

WHEN YOUR LIVING IN THE PAST
AND YOUR ROAD IS FAR AHEAD, AND YOU NEVER FINISH LAST
WHEN THE TRAIL ISN'T ROCKY
YOUR NOT SURE ABOUT THE PATH
BUT EVERYDAY THERE'S SMILES, AND YOUR LIVING JUST TO LAUGH
WHEN U WEREN'T WORRIED BOUT THE FAME, OR THROWING ALL THE CASH
WHEN WOMEN COULD JUST CHILL, YOUR NOT WORRIED ABOUT THE ASS
AND YOU WERE ADDING UP, BUT WASN'T WORRIED ABOUT THE MATH . . .
EVERYDAY SEEMED NEW, EVERY SKY SEEMED BLUE
AND NINTENDO AND TV, WAS EVERY AFTERNOON
NOW WE WATCH THE SUN, TURNOUT THE MOON
AND IM THINKING IF I COULD GO BACK
FROM WHEN I CAME OUT THE WOMB
WOULD I SWITCH IT UP?
TURN THE TABLES IN THE ROOM.

LIVING YOUNG

I DON'T THINK YOU CAN REALIZE
WAT IS GOIN THROUGH MY MIND
HOW DO I OBTAIN THIS SHINE
WITHOUT HAVING TO DO A LITTLE CRIME?
FRUSTRATING AINT IT?
YOU CAN FEEL SUCCESS SO BAD
YOU CAN FUCKIN TASTE IT
WHEN YOU CAN TOUCH THE CAKE SO MUCH
YOU CAN FUCKING BAKE IT
THE WORLD IS AT YOUR FINGER TIPS
SO GO AHEAD AND TAKE IT!
LIVE LIFE LIKE 2012
DON'T LIKE WHAT YOU SEE? YOU CAN GO TO HELL
GIRLS LOVE TO KISS AND TELL
DO IT BIG?
YUP, MIGHT ASWELL
I ,VE KISSED DEATH ON THE LIPS, STILL ALIVE TO TELL
HERE TO SET IT OFF!
CAN'T FUCK WITH AUTHORITY
SO IM MY OWN FUCKIN BOSS!
SO KEEP WANTING TO BE ONE
AND CONGRATULATE A REAL DUDE

WEN U FUCKIN SEE ONE!
A BILLIONAIRE, I WUD LOVE TO BE ONE
BUT UNTIL THE DAY IS HERE
IM JUST TRYING TO BE YOUNG

CROSS ROADS

LEFT OR RIGHT, RIGHT OR LEFT
YOU'RE AT THE CROSSROADS AND DON'T KNOW WHICH WAY IS BEST!
ON ONE HAND THE LEFT, MAKES U LOSE YOUR BREATH
THROUGH THICK N THIN, THROUGH PAIN N STRESS SO
WHAT IS RIGHT BOUT THE RIGHT?
COULD IT MAKE YOU CHANGE YOUR LIFE
THE WAY YOU FEEL, YOUR POINT AND SITE
SO WAT TO CHOOSE, WITH LEFT YOU CAN'T LOSE!
OR CAN YOU?
AND YET THE RIGHT IS A RISK
BUT IT CAN BE THE DIFFERENCE BETWEEN COMFORT AND BLISS . . .

MY MISSION

It's an emptiness
A void I can't avoid
A space of hate and misplaced
Anger and solitude
With the magnitude
To do more than I can do
It makes me rude
It makes me yell
I saw a preview of heaven
But have to live through hell
It makes me question
How on that day
I wasn't left where I would stay
If it means every night
I have to pray
In order to feel some peace
Where I may lay
And I ask why and question
The decision
to put my life on intermission
And with all do respect
and permission
If there even was a reason
And if so, then what was my MISSION?

THEY CAN'T REALIZE

They can't realize
That through my eyes I can see the a million days of deep blue sky
1000 miles through natures wild
And 100 times my senses
30 minutes pass the hour
And 20 years past the present
Words can't describe, the amount of pride
How it feels to battle sides
when both are you
And none can win
When you are you
But you're also him
In front of all to see
Standing alone
Wondering who can actually take me out of my zone
Change my perception
So my thoughts are not my own
and you are not the one
And I can see me growing old
with the one who just has won

Write n Pray

I've been battling a war
Since the day I was born
My mind, just reminds
All the shitt that was wrong
Every time I think about,
I really have to doubt it
That love's a special gift
Cause I can live without it
I walk alone
With a wall of stone
Feeling like
The only back I got
Is my own
Feeling lost
Just trying
To find my zone
Waiting for the day
That I'm truly home
But until that day
That I find my way
All I can do is
WRITE N PRAY!

AT THE END OF THE ROAD

WHOEVER SAID IT GETS EASIER WAS LYING
IT ONLY GETS HARDER!
THE ROAD GETS DARKER
THE PATH BREAKS AND CRACKS
YOU WATCH
AS THE LEAVES FROM THE DEAD TREES, COVER THE FLOOR
YOU LOOK UP
AT THE CLOUDY SKY, ASK THE USUAL WHY
CRY
AS THE RAIN DROPS POOR DOWN YOUR FACE
AND COVER THE TEARS
YOU LOSE BREATH
IF NOT FROM PAIN
THEN FROM FEAR
AND ALL YOU CAN DO IS HOPE
HOPE THAT YOU FIND THAT TREASURE,
AT THE END OF THE ROAD

WHY?

SO IF I KNEW THE ANSWER, I GUESS I WUDN'T TRY
WHY IS THE QUESTION, THE ANSWER IS WHY!
IT'S NEVER WRONG, IT NEVER LIES
IT DOESN'T MAKE SENSE, SO WHY EVEN TRY!
HOW MANY TIMES, CAN I SWALLOW MY PRIDE?
HOW MANY TIMES, CAN I ASK MYSELF?
HOW MANY TIMES, CAN I WISH
THE OUTCOME WILL CHANGE
WHEN I ALREADY TRIED
AND THE OUTCOME REMAINS!

YOUR JEWEL

YOU ARE BROKEN! YOU LOOK UP, AND THERE'S NOTHING LEFT!
YOUR TORN, MIND AND SPIRIT!
EMOTIONLESS AND DISTRAUGHT!
YOU ASK WHY? AND NO REPLY!
YOU QUESTION YOURSELF, YOUR ABILITY, AND YOUR EXISTENCE!
BUT DEEP DOWN, DEEP INSIDE YOU REALIZE SOMETHING
YOU HAVE A TREASURE! DEEP IN YOUR SOUL!
A JEWEL THAT CAN NEVER BE TAKEN!
THAT YOU KNOW BELONGS TO YOU AND ONLY YOU!
NEVER FORGET, THEY CAN TAKE IT ALL!
BUT THEY CAN'T TAKE THIS!
YOUR JEWEL! YOUR HEART!

RUST

HOW DO I FORGET, WHAT ARE THE STEPS?
AS I SIT AND REFLECT, I REALIZE MY NEGLECT
AND LACK OF RESPECT
BUT NO ONE IS PERFECT
BUT TIME WILL SHOW HOW WE GROW
AND AS I SPEAK THIS
I CAN SEE MY STRENGTH OUT OF MY WEAKNESS
AND HOW EACH OF US NEED TO TRUST
THAT IN THIS WORLD OF GREED AND LUST
WE CANT LET THE FEW THINGS THAT STILL SHINE . . .
RUST

ON THE DAYS

Fed up
with asking how come
Still I try again
Knowing what's the outcome
It's like
I'm breathing using one lung
An old soul
But always thought
That I would die young
And in life
You can second guess much
We work hard
For smooth sails
Still the roads rough
Is this truly love
Or is it just lust
The simple questions
But the answers so tough
A wild child
But believe it
I've done slowed up
The lord doesn't speak
But believe it

he has showed up
And ill take that
Over having no luck
That's all u got
On the days
You're feeling so stuck

THE BIG TOP

Welcome To the circus
Admission here is worthless
Being a clown to most
And elephant to some
Is your only purpose
Where women are candy
And you pay the price of purchase
There's people eating fires
Everyday you're crossing wires
Battling a freak show
With a bunch of Michael Meyers
Just making thru the lions
Hoping one day u retire
On the Big Top
And you entertained the world
Right before the show stopped . . .

WILL NEVER HAPPEN

I sit n think
As I stare at the wall
Reminisce on my pain
I've done been through it all
Is this the beginning of the end
can the luck finally change
Cause I've seen all I can see
From this world that is strange
from the lies n the fake
From the love n the hate
Never seeing what's real
Misunderstanding the deal
And through it all the hard work
I've lost my appeal
For a chance at romance
So I drink and I dance
All week party n such
And pretend I don't care
And don't give a fuck
Contemplate my actions
Despite its reaction
Truly believe one day
Ill be laughing

At each n every person
Who said your dreams
Are just that . . .
And will never happen

MAKES YOU MORE THAN A MAN

You took a piece
But you cudn't kill
That part of me
That leaves me in a place
Where I truly know
I ought to be
I've seen a lot
But I truly know
There was more to see
And you've see a lot
But know
there's truly more to me
And these words
could be taken for two
But if it makes sense . . .
Than it should be taken
For you
I remained tense
With the thought
This was the end
But I've remained since
So that thought was pretend.

Never been the same since
And I doubt that I can
But what doesn't break you
Makes you more than a man

HAMSTER WHEEL

LIKE THE HAMSTER WHEEL,
SPINNING WITH NO WHERE TO GO ROUND N ROUND
AND YET I'M STILL HERE BEYOND THE FEAR
BEYOND MY HOPES, IT SEEMS THAT WHAT I SEE DOESN'T CHANGE
PLASTIC TUBES, AND A CAGE . . .
WHEN WILL THE WHEEL STOP SPINNING
WHEN WILL I SEE A NEW BEGINING.
I RUN AND RUN
AND STILL END UP IN SQUARE ONE

Do You Make Mistakes?

I cry to myself . . .
Even though I feel
like its bad for my health
To much pride to cry
So I shut the world out
And keep it inside
I open your door
And realize . . .
You're not with me no more
And is it wrong
To question the Lord?
Even if he saved me before
He needs to save me some more
What does it take
I don't beg on the floor
Wouldn't question my faith
But I ask if it's true
That you don't make a mistake?

SEX

Sex . . .
The difference between loving someone, feeling someone, and kinda sorta
Sex . . .
A drug that costs nothing, and yet costs everything
Sex . . .
The devil and temptation?
Sex . . .
The reason we dress fly, smell right, and talk slick
Sex . . .
You want it before you start, question yourself after
Sex . . .
Feels better unprotected, but hurts if you don't!
Sex . . .
makes you self conscious, but can make you proud
Sex . . .
Can end relationships, or can strengthen them
Sex . . .
is Love?, or maybe just comfort
Sex . . .
Do you really need it? or can you do with just the orgasm?
Sex . . .

Can make someone pretty look ugly, and someone Ugly look a little more pretty
Sex . . .
Makes you feel incontrol, and for others out of control
Sex . . .
‡Is like a box of chocolates, never know what your gonna get·
Sex
Is liking opening up a gift on Christmas, after the surprise is done it's just a toy
Sex . . .
Usually better spontaneously
Sex
Can be the only reason to deal with the bullshitt!
Sex
The reason you can't let them go . . .
Sex
The reason they can't let you go . . .
Sex . . .
Who cares the reason, cause it's necessary!

DO YOU

IN THE END YOU GOTTA KNOW THE DIFFERNCE
BETWEEN FAMILY N FRIENDS
WORKERS N ASSOCIATES
THOSE THAT OWE, AND THOSE WHO DON'T REALLY OWE
YOU SHITT
LIFE AINT ALWAYS AN EASY CHICK
BUT YOU GOTTA LEARN HOW TO STROKE THE BITCH
SEE ME . . . I DO MY OWN THING
TREAT LIFE LIKE A GAME
AND JUST TRYING TO WEAR THE RING
TRYING TO DO WHAT'S RIGHT
AND CONSUMED BY MY SINS
SO SUMTIMES I TRY TO WRITE
MY WAY OUT OF THEM
I'M FAR FROM WHAT
THE PEOPLE SAY IS HIM!
LIKE I SAID, I JUST PLAY THE GAME
AND PLAY IT OUT TO WIN . . .
CUZ OUT HERE NO ONE CARES
ABOUT WHERE U'VE BEEN
OR WAT U'VE BEEN THRU
YOUR EVERDAY STRUGGLE
AND YOUR KIN TOO
SO DON'T WORRY BOUT THEM
AND JUSS WORRY HOW YOU DO U

Never Move Me

Yesterday is History
Tomorrow a Mystery
So all I can do is Pray
For Today
Through the skies
That are gray
I try to find
The light
Through my trials and tribulations
I try to do what's right
It seems like every night
I question what is life
And if I'm living wrong
Cause you can't live it twice
Through all the sacrifice
I feel I paid the price
The world is just a pie
I just want a slice
Until my day with Christ
The martyr of my movie
And u can cast your stones
But none can ever move me!

HOW TO GET IT BACK?

It's something I once had
Now I seem to lack
What do I have to do
To get that feeling back?
The smile . . .
That was brought by your face
When we would talk it out
While we stare into space
How to get that feeling back?
When the music is all around u
consumes your very soul
and your jumping out n shouting
Feeling out of control
How to get that feeling back?
When you would look at them
And feel that u can always trust
That they will always be there
That family's a must
How to get that feeling back?
When u really didn't need much
When just being you was great
When just just living life . . . was enough
How to get it back?

LIKE THE THINGS I OWN

HAUNTED BY MY PAST
USED TO BE LIKE, FUCK HOW I LOOK
LONG AS THE DUDES CAUGHT A LAUGH . . .
SURROUNDED BY THE TRASH
DID SOME SHITT I AINT PROUD OF, BUT FUCKIT . . . DID IT FOR THE CASH!
AND YOU CAN'T TURN BACK TIME
I DON'T LIVE WITH REGRET
BUT IT BE NICE TO TURN BACK MINE . . .
ERASE THE DAY, THAT CHANGED MY LIFE
DO RIGHT,BY THE GIRL I CALLED MY WIFE
AND FORGET ALL THOSE PEOPLE WHO AINT ‡DO ME RIGHT· . . .
SUMTIMES I JUSS WANNA LET OFF
RIGHT TO THE SKY
AND TAKE BACK THE WHATEVER I DENIED
TAKE BACK THE FOOLISH PRIDE
AND TAKE BACK THE THINGS THAT I ONCE SAID WERE MINE . . .
FUNNY HOW RANDOM PEOPLE SAY I'M CURSED
WITH A GIFT, THAT JUST HELPS TO MAKES SHITT WORSE
DEAL WITH CHICKS, WHO'S LIFE IS THEIR LOUIS PURSE
AND DUDES WHO PROLLY LIKE TO SEE ME HURT

PICTURES FILLED WITH 100'S OF BOTTLES N GIRLS . . .
BECAUSE OF THAT . . . EVERYONE ASSUMES THAT'S MY WORLD
NOT EVERYTHING THAT GLEAMS IS A PEARL
AND NOT EVERY CHICK U SEE IS MY GIRL!
THE MENTALITY OUT HERE . . .
DO WHAT U HAVE TO, JUSS TO MAKE SURE THAT YOU BALL
AND DUDES DO EACH OTHER, EVEN THOUGH THE HOOD IS TOO SMALL
NEED THE HOOKUP
ONLY TIME WHEN THE FEMALES CALL
AND I CAN GIVE A FUCK ABOUT IT ALL!
WEN I'M ON THE SIDE OF THE ROAD
LEFT ALL ALONE
I REALIZE, I'M ONLY AS GOOD AS THE THINGS I OWN

CAN'T HAVE IT ALL

You can have the clothes, girls, and cars
You can aim for the moon, but can't reach the stars
You can have all the friends, but never could tell who they are
but the only thing that is for certain,
you know you can go far . . .
to many memories of those you loved,
who turned into enemies, and empty hugs
you ask for the answers, from the one up above,
like why he got cancer, and the cure wasn't a drug
Maybe it isn't meant for you, for her to feel like you do
or anyone for that matter, but as long as you feel pain
the longer you can chatter . . .
and let the world see
what it takes for someone to be, what their destined to be . . .
So take you piece of the cake . . .
it taste good, even if it's small
and be glad that you have this . . .
cause you CAN'T HAVE IT ALL . . .

SMILE

LIKE I GOTTA REASON FOR IT?
SHORTY WENT AND BROKE YOUR HEART
WHEN YOU KNOW YOU SHUDVE STORED IT
SMILE
LIKE I GOTTA REASON FOR IT?
YOU'RE HAPPY THAT YOU'RE THREE MONTHS IN
FRIENDS SAYING GO ABORT IT
SMILE
CAUSE YOU REALLY WANT TO
BUT YOUR MAN JUST GOT SHOT
AND THERE'S NOTHING THEY CAN DO
SMILE
CAUSE YOU REALLY WANT TO
YOUR UNCLE DIAGNOSED WITH CANCER
AND HE'S GOING REAL SOON
SMILE
THEY SAY YOU LOOK BETTER WITH IT
TRYING FOR A JOB, BUT YOU CAN NEVER GET IT
SMILE
THEY SAY YOU LOOK BETTER WITH IT
CAUSE YOU WERE WAITING ON THAT CHANCE
BUT THEY SAID JUST FORGET IT
SMILE

CAUSE YOUR INFRONT OF FAMILY
BUT I CAN SMILE AT THEM, AND THEY NEVER SMILE BACK AT ME

SMILE
CAUSE YOUR INFRONT OF FAMILY
BUT THE ONLT TIME YOU SEE' EM IS WEDDINGS OR A TRAGEDY
SMILE
CAUSE YOUR ALIVE ANOTHER DAY
BUT SOME DUDES PLAYED WITH YOUR LIFE, AND NEVER HAD TO PAY
SMILE
CAUSE YOUR ALIVE ANOTHER DAY
BUT THEY'LL NEVER UNDERSTANDYOU
THEYLL NEVER SEE YOUR WAY
SMILE¿ WHY¿

DEATH

HAVE BECOME NUMB FROM THIS THING CALLED DEATH
I DON'T EVEN BOTHER TO SEE WHO PASSES ANYMORE
IT'S EXPECTED OUT HERE!
I MAKE ATLEAST ONE MONTHLY VISIT TO ORTIZ FUNERAL
IN A WORLD FULL OF VIOLENCE, GREED, DISEASE AND HATE
ATLEAST ONCE A WEEK SOMEONE YOU KNOW IS GOING TO PASS
I REMEMBER WHEN MY 6TH GRADE TEACHER DIED OF CANCER
I CRIED SO MUCH
IT WAS THE FIRST TIME SUMONE CLOSE TO ME HAD DIED
IT WAS SCARY
I REALIZED AT THAT POINT DEATH IS SOMETHING REAL
THAT YOU AREN'T HERE FOREVER
LITTLE BY LITTLE, MORE AND MORE
I GREW ACCUSTOMED TO IT
IF IT WASN'T A CAR ACCIDENT, SOMEONE GOT SHOT OR OVERDOSED . . .
IT'S SAD WE ALL START OUT SO INNOCENT
WE ASSUME GROWING UP
THAT EVERYONE IS GOING TO BE WHAT THEY WANT TO BE WHEN THEY GET OLDER . . .

BUT OUT OF 10
2 DROP OUT IN THE 10TH GRADE, 5 GO TO JAIL, AND 1 BECOMES A JUNKY . . .
THE REST ARE THE REST ARE THE CREAM OF THE CROP, AND WILL HOPEFULLY LIVE A FULL LIFE
IF CANCER, OR AIDS DON'T KILL THEM
OR IN MERLIN'S CASE WAR
THE WALLS ARE FULL OF RIP PICTURES, AND CANDLES
BUT NEXT WEEK NO ONE CARES, NO ONE REMEMBERS
JUST ANOTHER DEATH

No Matter . . .

NO MATTER HOW MUCH PRIDE
NO MATTER HOW I LIVE
NO MATTER HOW I DIE
I CAN LIVE WITH THE FACT
HOW HARD I TRIED
TO MAKE IT WORK
TO STOP THE CRIES
TO STOP THE PAIN
TO STOP THE LIES
TO FEEL THE SAME
TO DRY YOU'RE EYES
AND NO ONE SEES
WHAT THE WORLD HAS DONE TO ME
HOW IT CHANGED MY SOUL
HOW I PLAY SO YOUNG
BUT I THINK SO OLD
HOW MY HEART TO COLD
SO I'M LIVING WITH THE DOUBT
THAT EVEN IF I COULD
NO ONE SEES WHAT I'M ABOUT
WHAT DOES IT TAKE TO ERASE THE HATE
TO FIND MY PLACE

TO HEAR ME SPEAK
TO FEEL THE SAME
TO LEAVE THESE STREETS
AND FIND THAT PEACE

ISN'T ENOUGH

I'm 26, and I ask myself this
What is LOVE, does it even exist?
Is the price of a house, worth more than what you feel from a kiss
Can a bank account get all your wrongs dismissed?
Is Love what makes it all feel right?
or is Love simply realizing this is LIFE!
Is the physical what's most appealing?
would you still LOVE me, if there were leaks in our ceiling?
Is it my touch, that brings you our healing?
or is it just that I gave you the bag you were needing?
And you can put up with my antics . . .
as long as you're eating
Each day I grow colder, it's like my soul is bleeding
Cause I realize my question's repeating
‡Is that all that matters?·
and if I got to keep asking
than the answer is yes
and it truly doesn't matter if together, your best!
The reason your stuck
isn't your luck . . .
LOVE does exist
it just isn't enough . . . .

Never Grows

I shoot myself in the foot
I always find, when I never look
Try to give the benefit of the doubt
But to forget the past . . .
Is just not what I'm about
It's so hard to let go
With the thought of pursuing
Despite what you know
And u feel a certain way
but u can't let it show
Until further notice
They are all full of shitt
that's just how it goes
from the games n their stories
to their walk n their pose
so I put the wall up
and my love never grows
so why do I wonder
why I'm alone? . . .

Let He Without Sin

Let he without sin,
Cast the first stone
The oppression of a prince
On his quest for the thrown
And it's a battle fought
All on his own
A war with his demons
Just to make his way home
Man on a mission
They hate the lifestyle
But respect the ambition
Never takes orders
Just his own intuition
Never follows the recipe
The chef of his kitchen
Under constant scrutiny
Of who he is
And who he's supposed to be
Like the persecution
of the man on his rosary
They can crucify him to death
But in the end he resurrects

When You're Trying to Be a Boss . . .

Never felt like anyone understood
How u can stand in a room of wolves,
And still keep it hood
Out here were destined for no good
And then your hated on,
When u try to show the goons
That we could
Be something more
Than the runners of a spot
Owner of a liquor store,
Thugs posted on a block.
They give u funny looks
When they see u suited up,
You tell the CEO, u went to college . . .
And he don't give a fuck
So what the fuck is up?
Is this a no win?
Can u keep it real,
Still be a success
Without trying to be them?
Or both worlds can't co-exist?
do you just get lost?
Can you have friends,
When you're trying to be a BOSS?

Deceitful Eyes

My mind is at a stand still
An emptiness within
But still I keep my hands filled
With doubt and concern
Some was misfortune
Others I earned
Mistakes I've made
But never could learn
Emotions and fire
That never could burn
Wondering n wanting
For my chance
For my turn
Did it pass me by
I sit and I wonder why
By day I smile
At night I cry
Battle my inner truths
And display my outer lies
To a never ending supply
Of sly hearts
And deceitful eyes

PART 2

LOVE

FORGIVE AND FORGET

THEY SAY . . .
THE KEY TO HAPPINESS IS TO FORGIVE N FORGET
I SAY . . .
THE KEY TO HAPPINESS, LIVING WITHOUT A SHRED OF REGRET
AND I DONT JUST FORGIVE . . .
FOR THE SAKE OF FORGET
CAUSE YOU DID ME REAL BAD SO I AIN'T FORGIVING YOU YET . . .
BLAME IT ON WATEVER . . .
ADULTS WORK WITH RESPECT . . .
AND IF YOU WORKING REAL HARD
YOU SHOULD BE RECEIVING A CHECK
YOU SHUDN'T BE WORKING,
JUSS TO BE RECEIVING NEGLECT
CUZ I DID U RIGHT . . .
MAN I GAVE U MY BEST . . .
IN LIFE
YOU WILL FIND THAT'S YOU WORK THROUGH ALL THE TESTS
AND SOMETIMES . . .
IN THE END YOU CAN WORK THROUGH ALL THE STRESS
YOU TRY AND PICKUP WHAT YOU FEEL YOU GOT LEFT

AND YOU GO BEYOND JUST ALL THE KISSES N SEX
AND YET
ALL THAT LEFT IS SOME SMURKS N SUM PECKS . . .
AND YOU FEEL
YOU GOTTA TRY WHATEVER IS NEXT . . .
IT IS WHAT IT IS . . .
JUST BE GLAD THAT YOU'RE LIVING AND BLESSED
AND EVERYDAY YOU LIVE AGAIN.
WITH A CHANCE TO DO IT TO DEATH!

KNEW IT ALL

BABY I MISS U MORE N MORE EVERYDAY
YOU CAN TAKE MY SUN AWAY
AND TURN MY SKY'S INTO GREY
OR U CAN MAKE IT BRIGHTER!
IT'S LIKE EVERY TIME I SEE YOU
I WANNA HOLD YOU A LITTLE TIGHTER
WHERE DID WE GO WRONG¿
THAT GIVES ME THE INSPIRATION
TO WRITE TOO MANY SONGS
LIFE IS A JOURNEY
AND THE JOURNEY SEEMS TO LONG
AND WE DID EACH OTHER GOOD
SO WHY DO IT FEEL SO WRONG¿
BUT ITS LIKE EVERY TIME WE KICK IT
I FEEL I CAN CHANGE THE PAST,
GO BACK N FIX . . .
YOU AND ME WAS A HIT . . .
LETS GO BACK, REMIX IT!
PRIZE OUT A RAFFLE
GO ON, GRAB YOUR TICKET
WEN I LOOK IN TO YOUR EYES
YOU MADE ME DROP MY PRIDE
ON THE NIGHTS YOU OPENED UP

MADE A DUDE WANNA CRY
AND WE DON'T TELL NO LIES
THE PICTURE SAYS IT ALL
LIKE SOLDIERS IN ATTENTION
OUR LOVE IS STANDING TALL
AND I DON'T GOT DRESS THIS FLY,
OR SHOW U HOW I BALL
NEVER HAD TO SAY NO WORDS
U ALREADY KNEW IT ALL

IT'S WRONG . . .

IF IT'S WRONG, WHY DO IT FEEL SO RIGHT?
WHY DO WE LIVE BY DAY, N DREAM AT NIGHT?
WHY CAN'T IT BE THE WAY IT WAS . . .
WHY CAN'T IT GO BACK TO THE KISS N HUGS
AND WHO INVENTED THIS THING CALLED LOVE?
WHY CAN'T WE TURN BACK THE HANDS?
I WAS A BOY THEN, BUT NOW I'M A MAN
WHY CUDN'T IT BE? WHY CUDN'T I SEE?
AND JUST LOWERED MYSELF
ENOUGH TO SHOW, WAT I TRULY FELT . . .
AND GO BACK TO THE WAY IT WAS . . .
AND WHO THE FUCK WANTED THIS THING CALLED LOVE.

WHO WOULD PAINT YOUR WALL?

WHEN YOU'RE STUCK BETWEEN THE TWO,
AND YOU DON'T KNOW WHAT TO DO . . .
SAY YOU NEED A LITTLE TIME,
BUT YOUR EYES CAN SEE THE PROOF
YOU'RE LIVING THROUGH A LIE,
AND YOUR HEART CAN FEEL THE TRUTH
YOU GO AGAINST YOUR PRIDE,
HOPING YOU WON'T LOSE
WHICH WAY YOU'RE GOING TO CHOOSE?
ONE'S KIND OF SPECIAL,
AND THE OTHER'S IN YOUR SHOES . . .
ONE IS YESTERDAY'S PAPER,
THE OTHER IS THE NEWS . . .
ONE HAS MADE YOU CRY,
THE OTHER IS YOUR MUSE . . .
AND THAT'S JUST LIFE . . .
WE ALWAYS WANT WHAT JUST AINT RIGHT
WE ALWAYS NEED WHATS WORTH LESS THAN THE PRICE
AND ALWAYS WANT TO BATTLE . . .
WHAT WE SHUDN'T BE THINKING TWICE . . .
THE ANSWER IS RIGHT INFRONT, BUT YOU STILL DON'T KNOW
WHAT IT IS YOU WANT, AND IT SHUDN'T BE THAT HARD

BUT YOU KNEW IT WOULD BE FROM THE START . . .
YOUR LIFE IS JUST LIKE ART . . .
PAINT IT HOW YOU WANT TO
AND DON'T EVER HESITATE,
OVER SOMEONE WHO DOESN'T WANT YOU!
LIFE IS JUST TO SHORT,
THE WORLD IS JUST TO SMALL
TO NOT TAKE A CHANCE,
ON THE ONE WHO'D PAINT YOUR WALL . . .

1000 DEATHS

BETTER MAKE A DECISION
BEFORE THE MOVIE BEGINS
AND YOU'RE LIVING AN INTERMISSION
CONTEMPLATED MY DECISIONS
I CAN ADMIT THAT . . .
BUT THAT DON'T GIVE U THE RIGHT
TO JUST FEEL YOU CAN STRIKE BACK
TIME ISN'T GOING TO STAND STILL
NEITHER WILL I . . . BUT YOU WILL
BE LIVING ANOTHER LIE . . .
IF U THINK I'M GOING TO LAY DOWN AND DIE . . .
REFUSE TO BE ANOTHER OPTION!
LIFE IS PASSING YOU BY . . .
AND FOR SURE I'M NOT STOPPING
SO YOU BETTER PROCEED WITH CAUTION,
HAD OTHER CHOICES . . . BUT NOW YOU LOST ONE
FEELING LIKE YOU TRULY GOT THE POWER
WHEN WHAT YOU REALLY GOT IS A PROBLEM . . .
THE SECOND YOU REALIZE . . . THAT I'M NOT THERE TO SOLVE THEM
GOT A PLAN B? WELL GO AHEAD AND CALL HIM . . .
CAUSE THE WORLD IS HARD, AND BELIEVE I'VE SEEN TOO MUCH

TO JUST TAKE A LOSS . . . AND FEEL LIKE GIVING UP
MIGHT HAVE BEEN THE BEST . . .
OR ATLEAST MORE THAN ALL THE REST
BUT LIFE IS TO SHORT . . . TO BE LIVING A 1000 DEATHS!

REWIND

EACH TIME THE PAIN IS LESS, AND LESS
CAUSE YOU LIVE WITH THE FACT
THAT YOU TRIED YOUR BEST . . .
BUT YOU RUNNING A CIRCLE
TILL YOU HAVE NO BREATH
TO YOUR LEGS GIVE OUT
AND YOU HURT YOUR CHEST . . .
AND YOU ASK YOURSELF AGAIN
IS THIS INEVITABLE
IS EVERY RELATIONSHIP REGRETTABLE
OR IS THERE ONE THAT WILL LAST FOR UNFORGETTABLE?
IS THERE SOMEONE FOR EVERYONE?
IF SO SHOW ME THE WAY . . .
CAUSE I'D RATHER TAKE THE BENCH
WITH THE SILLY GAMES YOU PLAY . . .
AND YET I CHOSE TO STAY . . .
AND IGNORE THE YIELD SIGN . . .
INSTEAD I HIT THE PEDAL
THINKING ITS OUR TIME . . .
BUT MAYBE THE MOVIES DONE
AND THIS IS SIMPLY A REWIND

YOUR EYES TALK

YOUR EYES SAY ENOUGH!
WHAT YOUR WORDS DON'T!
FEAR AND CONFUSION
FEAR OF GETTING HURT . . .
BUT TELL ME WHAT IS WORSE?
SECOND GUESSING WHAT YOU FEEL
OR HOPING TIME WILL HEAL?
AT THE END OF THE DAY
YOU KNOW WHAT U FEEL IS REAL!
AND THAT WHAT IS RIGHT
IS MEANT TO BE
WHERE THERE IS YOU
THERE WILL ALWAYS BE ME!

PICTURE

Look at the picture
wish I could just kiss her
remember the girl,
boy how I miss her
shared my love like a wife
held me down like a sister
as much as I NEED her
wish I can dismiss her
Cause the mark was too strong
and I try to hold on
hear your voice in my head
See your face in a song
Do you feel the same way¿
Wish we could undo the wrong¿
Underneath all the pain
does that LOVE still remain¿
I know my life needs a change
Cause I'm done with the game
Could retire the crown
left my mark on this town
but u left a mark on my heart
the bout was more than a round
Willing to risk
If it means I cud relive the kiss
and remake the pic

Protect Me from Myself

Protect me from myself
Not the women
Or the wealth
My life at times
Ain't conducive to my health
But maybe u can
Protect me from myself
From self-destruction
My harsh decisions
Never think the repercussion
But life ain't come
With these instructions
The only thing that motivates
Is bass n percussion
At times
I can't take the negative
Out my mind
And I sit and rewind
And think its only time
Before I succumb to the signs
But maybe u can save me
Not from them
But the things that have made me
I don't know how to react

WORTH BEING CONFUSED

It's like I take a step foward
and you take two back . . .
What do I do
to see this through
Change my plan of attack?
As a matter of fact
I feel I couldn't find you
if you were part of a map
not everything is white and black
they're are shades of gray
and lord knows . . .
I have paved the way . . .
to try to make this work
tired of the games you play
and you say I'm a jerk?
damn that hurts!
and then you act like its nothing . . .
but I'm not a mind reader,
and you didn't come with instructions
just wish you would stop your fronting
and realize you got something to lose
at the end of the day . . .
I won't figure you out
but can figure if it's worth being confused!

Trust n Lust

THEY SAY IN GOD WE TRUST
BUT IF I DO IT FOR YOU,
IT WAS ALL JUST LUST?
YOU'RE BEAUTIFUL, THAT'S ALWAYS A PLUS
BUT DEEP DOWN
YOUR HEART IS CONSUMED WITH HATE AND RUST
USED AND OVER WORN
AND STILL YOU PURSUE, EVEN THOUGH YOU HAVE BEEN WARNED
YOU CAN'T HELP IT . . .
YOUR HEART TOO HAS BEEN TORN
AND YOU HOPE TO MEND IT BACK
WITH THE WORDS THAT SHE HAS SWORN . . .
TO NEVER LEAVE YOUR SIDE
AND YOU'VE SEEN A FEW THINGS TO WORRY ABOUT
BUT STILL YOU LET THEM SLIDE . . .
IT'S HARD TO BEAR . . .
YOU'RE A MAN WITH PRIDE
AND ALL YOU CAN DO IS SMILE
CAUSE MEN NEVER CRY!
AND IS THIS WHAT RELATIONSHIPS ARE FOR?
IS THIS BETTER FROM WHERE YOU WERE BEFORE?
BECAUSE NOW YOU CAN SAY YOU HAVE COMPANY . . .
BUT WHAT YOU REALLY NEED IS MORE . . .

Hoping there is more

Never thought I could feel
The same way twice
The first time was good
But I paid the price
Daddy said u ain't a man
Till u experience life
And a man can't be a man
If he isn't held right
By his wife
Was it the circumstance?
Or the fullness of the moon
That took away my breath
And lit up the whole room
Want to feel its right
Or am I just destined for doom
Can it really work
Is it moving to soon?
Questions can't be answered
Like why is the sky blue
And there's no cure for cancer
All I know is I feel right
When your in my presence
And u just rubbing on my head

Makes me feel so pleasant . . .
So maybe its just a moment
But it won't last
Maybe I'm just pretending
And were still stuck up on our past . . .
But this I know for sure
You opened up a door
And I am stepping through
Hoping that there's more . . .

The Fire

You put your hand on the fire
Knowing that it burns
But you're thinking that it won't
Hoping it's your turn . . .
To change your dilemma
From the lessons
You have learned
But in the end u can't pretend
You like getting burned
You can't help it . . .
Its and attraction
A certain satisfaction
That you fight a losing battle
Always with the same
course of action
You already know the results
And still u will proceed
Cause you feel that this fire
Gives you all you need
You're addicted to it bad
Gives you a high like some weed
But in the end you take a crash
Like you had sum speed.

So when will it stop
When will you not give in
When will you give
You're hand a rest
And never let it burn again . . .

FOR REAL?

So this is what it is?
I want to make it right
With you
You're having someone else kid?
On the days I used to fantasize
About the crib, and seeing a mini me
Bottle n a bib
Now I got to let you live?
My heart hurts
With the thought
Of u starting a fam
With another man
On the other hand
I have to know
Things happen for a reason
Even if deep down u can't
Believe them
Only thing we know for sure
Is the changing of the seasons
And the odds are never with you
You just got to beatem!
So hope I can find peace
in the motivation

From life
You and the street
The words that I speak
Can move those that I know,
Love and have yet to meet

You and I

The mind already knows
What the heart can't see
Why it feels so right
And yet can't be
Why day and night
I can't sleep
Why I feel so old
My pain so deep
Words can't speak
What your eyes do say
That our moment isn't now
But of course one day
And that through it all
We would find our way
The picture isn't perfect
But was meant to stay
And I can't deny
Thoughts of a different portrait
Brings tears to my eyes
I was living out a plan
But my plan was made of lies
And now I'm feeling kind of empty
With a pain that won't subside

So ask myself the questions
And my response is always why?
But the question isn't simple
What is YOU AND I

Will Never Be

What you want
Isn't always what you need
Your heart is so cold
But still has time to bleed
The hate just ripens
Like fruit growing from a seed
And in the end
You see it will never be
You have another option
But it ain't your cup of tea
You tell her what it is
But she sees it differently
You're making good music
Like a symphony
But in the end
U see it will never be
So you ride the waves
Looking out to sea
Wishing what u wanted
Was truly what u need
But it truly wasn't
And you have to see
that in the end
it will never be

WHERE GOOD THINGS LIVE

Every time I think about it
Kills me inside
On the nights you would
Sit there and cry
I'd dry your eyes
Telling you everything is all right
And now it's like those tears
Were all just a lie
I see a child . . .
And the things that go
Through my mind
Did I deny the truth
The fact . . .
you weren't mine for sometime
but every time you said
You loved me
I would rewind
To a place that wasn't ugly
When we were one of a kind
What else can be said
But it is what it is
And one day
Ill see a little me in a crib

And ill sit and reminisce
On the things that we did
And hope it has its place
Where good things
Always live . . .

The Sequel

Each day I wake up
It's always on my mind
Why the script
Was rewritten
The actors and the lines
Change of direction
Production and the stars
Dinner and a movie
Turned to smiles
From a far
A new supporting cast
You said the old would never pass
You said the movie was a masterpiece
And would always last
Romance and a tragedy
But could always make you laugh
A critic's choice
That would be praised
By the people
But now Part 2
Is another actor's SEQUEL . . .

FEELIN AINT THE SAME

You leave the door cracked
Enough for a lil hope
It's been about 3 months
Since the last time we spoke
And the sigth of your name
On my caller I'd
kinda makes me choke
I stare at the ceiling
Like damn . . . wish this was all a joke
But it ain't
n I'm waiting
For the picture your going to paint
Sure enough your sorry for what happened
Wishing things were different
Always thought it be a fairy tale
But it always isn't
Saying that you love me
N always need me as a friend
When knowing what we had Will never be again
And a part of me hurts
Hearing your in pain
And the other half is rough
Doesn't even change

Cause no matter what is said
The fact still remains
That I am not the one
And the feeling ain't the same

Never True

To busy looking ahead of you
To notice what was in front of you
Dealt with 2 personalities
Even if there was just 1 of you
Cudn't see myself without
Now it's like I want none of you
But accept the good
With the bad is all
that I'm gonna do
Cause to lie and say
That I hate each day
that the smiles
N laughs
Didn't make their
Way
To change my mind
On yesterday
On before you said
You were here to stay
And now its like a distant memory
And I wonder if you remember me
The way I remember you
On the days we swore

That we'd live it through
And even if I say
I wish it never was
It's NEVER TRUE

WHATS GOING DOWN

From the start up
I swore I'd keep my guard up
But each day it gets harder
When I look into your eyes
I think I should be your baby's father
And more than that . . .
Partner and confidant
But whenever things get serious
you act nonchalant
Switch things up
In front of an ambiance.
Can't figure it out
What is it exactly that you want?
Cause me
I'm sure of what I need
Not the fame or the greed
But one who's necessary
As the very air I breathe
Who's willing to see
This fruit grow from out this seed
Tell me let u be
Then miss when I'm not around
So please let me know
What exactly is going down?

Stay on My Grind

The saddest feeling
Is knowing I'm alone
And then I start the reading
Get all up in my zone
It's like every other word
Stops my breathing
My heart skips a beat
You say it's me your needing
But still I'm not believing
And I ask myself
How and why
And I continue reading
On how u hurt n cry
How deep down
What you felt inside
Was that . . . It was always me
And eventually
We would always be
And its so cliche
But what else can one say?
What's done is done
God wanted it that way
I have to much pride

To live a lie
the story forever changed
something's . . .
will never be the same
so if they say what's meant to be
with stands the test of time
then I guess time will tell
Until then . . .
STAY ON MY GRIND

PART 3

THEM

JEREMY

PEOPLE ASK, IF THERE IS A GOD . . .
WHY IS THERE SO MUCH BAD IN THE WORLD . . .
WHY ARE THE MONSTERS, RAPISTS, MURDERS . . . ETC.
MOST OF ALL, WHY DO THE GOOD DIE YOUNG . . .
I'M NOT GOING TO LIE AND SAY THAT I HAVEN'T QUESTIONED GOD . . .
HIS EXISTENCE OR HIS REASONS . . . BUT ONE THING I TRULY BELIEVE IN MY HEART
IS THIS . . .
THAT EVERYTHING HAS PURPOSE, EVERYTHING HAS A REASON . . .
LIFE ISN'T MEANT TO BE QUESTIONED . . .
AND I AM BLESSED WITH THE ABILITY TO BELIEVE AND HAVE FAITH.
I HAVE SEEN GOD, I KNOW HE EXISTS . . .
I SEE HIM ALL THE TIME IN LITTLE SIGNS . . .
WHEN SOMEONE MAKES ME SMILE, WHEN I'M FEELING DOWN
ON THE DAYS I WAS BROKE! AND HIT THE BANK FOR A QUICK $100.
MOST OF ALL I SEE HIM EVERYDAY, IN MY GRANDMA . . .
WHO WITHOUT HER BLESSING . . .
I MIGHT NOT HAVE BEEN HERE TODAY!

THE OTHER DAY I SAW HIM AGAIN . . .
SOME ONE OUT OF NOWHERE, TOLD ME . . . ‡YOU KNOW HE'S OK, AND THAT HE'S WITH YOU EVERY STEP YOU TAKE!·
ANYONE WHO HAS GOTTEN CLOSE TO ME KNOWS, I HAVE A BIG WALL . . . AND ONLY ALLOW PEOPLE TO SEE . . . WHAT I WANT THEM TOO . . .
THIS WASN'T A RANDOM PERSON . . . BUT IT WASN'T SOMEONE THAT KNOWS ME ENOUGH TO KNOW THE DETAILS OF MY LIFE . . .
TO KNOW MY THOUGHTS, WHAT I FEAR . . . WHAT I DESIRE . . .
BUT I FOUND COMFORT IN HER WORDS, AND ACCEPTED IT . . . AS ANOTHER SIGN THAT THE LORD ASSURES ME THAT HE HEARS ME . . . HE WALKS WITH ME . . .
AND THAT I HAVE A COUPLE ANGELS . . . IN MY FRIENDS AND LOVE ONES WHO HAVE PASSED!
AND THAT MY UNCLE IS AT REST, AND SUFFERED . . . BUT NOW HE SMILES FOR ETERNITY . . .

MERLIN

START TO JOT IT DOWN, BEFORE I GET SOBER
I MISS MY DUDE, AS I GET OLDER
I'M NOT THE MAN YOU KNEW, NOW I'M WAY COLDER
DAMN, HOW IT HURTS . . . WHY THE LORD HAD TO TAKE
YOU MERK?
COCKY DUDE . . .
ALWAYS TALKED LIKE YOU WAS MOVING WEIGHT
ALL UP IN THE TEEN BASH DOIN A ‡HARLEM SHAKE·
IN YOUR EYES I COULD SEE LOVE AND HATE
FOR THE HOOD, KNOWING ONE DAY YOU'D ESCAPE . . .
PAPER BANDANNA AND BLUE CHUCKS
WHITE-T TO YOUR KNEES
YOU AINT GIVE A FUCK
YOU CALLED EVERYONE ‡YOUR SON·
HAD AN INFATUATION WITH GUNS
AND ALWAYS SAID SOMEDAY
YOU'D BUST SUM!
HAD BIG DREAMS!
ALWAYS WANTED TO BE A MARINE
WE TALKED ABOUT IT AT NAIROBI'S SWEET 16 . . .
I TOLD YOU, YOU'RE JUST A FIEND . . . LET IT GO!
AND ONE DAY YOU'D LIVE TO BE OLD
BUT U LIVED YOUR DESTINY!

AND I CAN REFLECT ON THE TIMES
YOU BROUGHT OUT THE BEST OF ME
HAD THE FLAVOR!
WE'RE ALL JUST JOCKIN OUT YOUR RECIPE!
AHEAD OF YOUR TIME
LIKE MOST OF US, DABBLED IN CRIME
BUT ALWAYS NEW ONE DAY YOU WOULD SHINE . . .
SO U DID AND STILL DO!
YOUR STORY AINT FINISHED WE GOT TO LIVE IT THROUGH . . .
I BELIEVE THIS IS TRUE
YOU'RE SHARING A CLOUD WITH A.J. AND JEREMY TOO!
AND PROMISE TO NEVER NEGLECT
CAN LOOK UP THE BLOCK NOW
AND NEVER FORGET!
LOVE YOU!

JR

My greatest fear is becoming you
Miserable, frustrated with the feeling
There's nothing you can do
Talk like you were destined for pain
And sometimes I hear you speak
And feel like are destiny's the same
You could never understand me
Probably never will
And yet I always understood you
And I regret sum decisions that I made too
But still I keep faith . . .
That underneath the grey lines, the sky's blue
We share a similar start . . .
Identical, even in body language
And an unconditional heart
Love for the wrong women, as well for the arts
So I hope you can believe
That one day it can all change
That you can find peace
And I do the same . . .

Love Without Regrets

Don't even know where to begin
How the story changed
Once was all I had
But now nowhere the same
I question time and time again
How could you let it happen?
Was the price of the beauty
Greater than your duty
To always protect me
Said I never have to fear
And you had left me
To care for myself
Was not having me
equal more than the wealth?
And can't you see we were happier
Before it was there
When tomorrow wasn't certain
And lived without care
And did it take for you to lose it
For you to realize
Who is still there?
Pains me, though I love you
With all due respect

Maybe one day I'll forgive
But never forget
And we could move past
And love without any regrets

For you, a Letter

I'm writing you a letter
Wish I can say most of this in person
But I always could write things
Much better
I wish you didn't have to see half of what you did
I wish that we spoke more when you were a little kid
I wish I could tell you the truth
from the get
I pray that even though, you never felt neglect
And I know you know, you're all I truly have
And I pray that the good, truly out ways the bad
At times I see you sad . . .
Probably wonder if things were the opposite
How would you live
But you'd be the same you on the other side of the bridge
so just stay positive . . .
continue your path
and I pray that smiles never fades
and your happiness lasts . . .

In His Glory

My angel on Earth
The only thing consistent
Since the day of my birth
I watch you cry . . .
And can't describe all your pain
Just waiting for a sign
To know he was saved . . .
Your faith makes you brave
And able to with stand
You hold the world's heart, in the palm of your hands
Saved me from death
Blessed me with love
Made me realize
There's truly someone watching above
and I don't show emotions
never one to say it out loud
but I will complete your wish
to see me happy n proud.
And the only thing I'm certain of
That at the end of the story
You and the rest
Will reunite in HIS GLORY . . .

EPILOGUE

Well there you have it. I figure people can relate more to emotions, than actual facts. The most consistent of which being your own self image, and how that transcends through everything else. This was just the first chapter.

This story is still being written . . . the hill is still being climbed. I hope and pray through my trials and tribulations, I can find my ultimate goal of peace. That is all I truly desire! Though I'm only a little over a quarter century in age, I have lived double if not triple. I have seen things, only scripted in movies. I have loved someone more than I felt I could love myself, only to realize that will never bring satisfaction. I have had my ups and downs with family, only to strengthen my own self-worth. One realizes at the end of the day, you live your life and no one else's. You can't depend someone will care for you as much as you care for yourself. You can only hope, they respect you as much as you do them. Finally, you have to be able to look yourself in the mirror, and be content with what you see. Nobody's perfect, life is far from easy. All you can do is try, and pray for a better tomorrow. Take each day's lessons into the next. You have faith that everything truly does happen for a reason.

Ultimately, what I want you to take above anything else . . . is that no matter where you come from . . . no matter your background . . . rich or poor . . . city or country, we as human beings share in the same internal and external struggles each and every day. The two teenagers from the city sharing a slice of pizza on a park bench, is no different from the two on a porch at a farm in Kansas. I'm sure everyone battles their own demons, and questions themselves. I'm sure everyone has battled with trust in others and loved ones. Love is Love, Pain is Pain, Life is Life . . . it's all the same!

www.ingramcontent.com/pod-product-compliance
Ingram Content Group UK Ltd.
Pitfield, Milton Keynes, MK11 3LW, UK
UKHW041934190726
13854UKWH00004B/1581

9 781463 409999